The Children of
MAURITANIA

THE WORLD'S CHILDREN

The Children of
MAURITANIA
Days in the Desert and by the River Shore

LAUREN GOODSMITH

Carolrhoda Books, Inc./Minneapolis

*To the children and the families, who made this book possible;
and to my parents, who have made everything possible.*

Library of Congress Cataloging-in-Publication Data

Goodsmith, Lauren.

    The children of Mauritania : days in the desert and at the river
shore / Lauren Goodsmith.
       p.   cm. – (The World's children)
    Includes index.
    Summary: Follows the lives of two children from two of
Mauritania's cultural groups : a Moorish girl and a Halpoular boy.
    ISBN 0-87614-782-1
    1. Mauritania–Social life and customs–Juvenile literature.
2. Family life–Mauritania–Juvenile literature. [1. Mauritania–
Social life and customs. 2. Family life–Mauritania.] I. Title.
II. Series: World's children (Minneapolis, Minn.)
DT554.4.G66   1993
966.1–dc20   92-46145
                                                          CIP
                                                           AC

Manufactured in the United States of America

1 2 3 4 5 6 – P/JR – 98 97 96 95 94 93

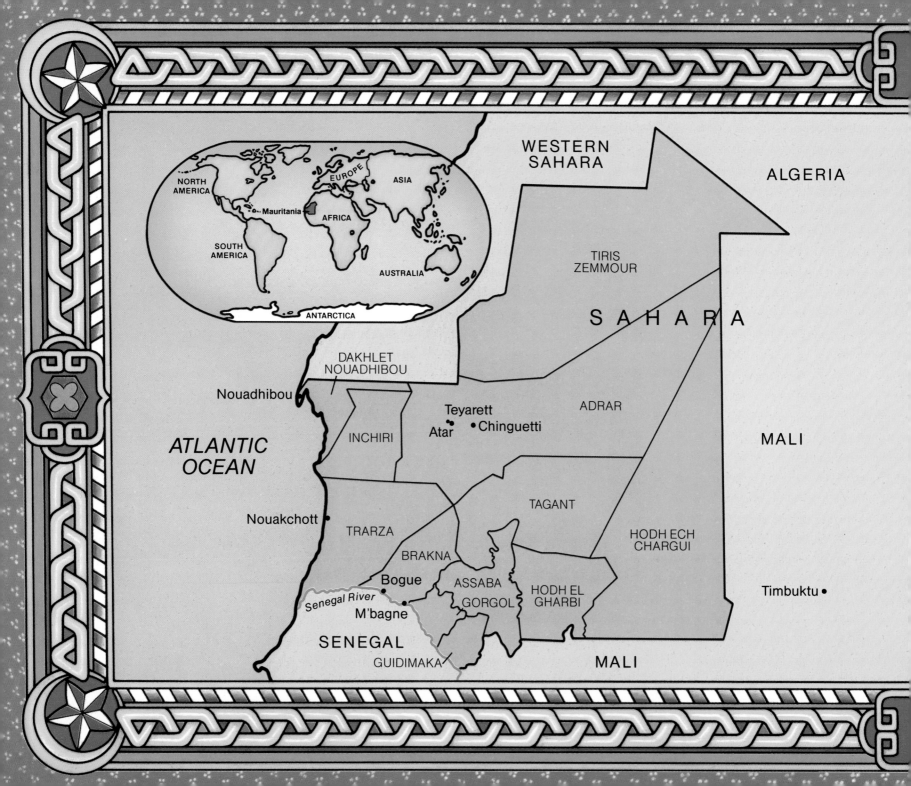

Introduction

Mauritania is a land where North and West Africa meet. The Sahara Desert, as it stretches toward the south, merges into the flat grassland known as savannah; here, sandy dunes become fertile soil. Across these contrasting zones, Arab and black African cultures interact.

Long ago, caravans carrying gold, ivory, salt, and slaves crossed the Sahara from the city of Timbuktu into what is now Morocco. Prosperous cities rose along the trading routes, which were controlled by the Berbers—nomadic people who were early inhabitants of the region. When Arab tribes came to North Africa in the seventh and eighth centuries, they brought their language and their religion, Islam; these were eventually adopted by the Berbers. The Mauritanian city of Chinguetti, now half-covered by sand, became a famous center of religious learning; it is one of the seven holy cities of Islam.

The Moors, the country's largest ethnic group, are descendants of both the Arab and the Berber people. They speak a language called Hassaniya that is a kind of Arabic with many Berber words mixed into it. Traditionally desert dwellers, they have lived mostly in the northern and central parts of the country.

The majority of Mauritania's black African people belong to one of three ethnic groups: the Halpoular, the Wolof, or the Soninke. While they all share the same faith in Islam, each group has its own language and culture. *Halpoular* means "the people who speak the Poular language." Black African Mauritanians have always lived mostly in the south, in the fertile valley of the Senegal River. They have been farmers, herders, and fishermen there for centuries.

Years of drought and the growth of the desert have made changes in the land and in the way of life of most Mauritanians. Many have moved from the countryside and villages to the big cities and towns. There are others, however, who still live in the same places and in much the same way that they always have.

These are scenes from the lives of two Mauritanian children from very different parts of the country—a Moor girl of the northern desert, and a Halpoular boy of the southern river valley.

*O*ut in the desert, in a valley beyond the village of Teyarett, there is a white tent. Fatimatou lives here, with her mother, father, sister, and brothers.

Their tent is made of cool cotton, pale on the outside but full of bright colors inside. Fatimatou's mother stitched it together out of many different pieces of cloth. The floor of the tent is made of large woven mats that cover the sand and can be moved around like rugs. An *amshaka*—a kind of high table with carved wooden legs—holds most of the family's belongings.

Nearby is the tent of Fatimatou's older brother, his wife, and their two children; another tent, just a short walk away, is the home of some of the family's friends.

Fatimatou's family's tent (opposite page and above)

Above: *Fatimatou saying her morning prayers.* Below: *Beetles left these trails in the desert sand.*

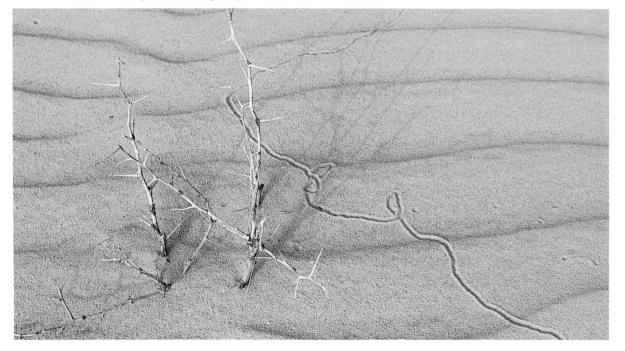

The desert is very quiet in the early morning when Fatimatou wakes up to say her prayers. She and her family are Muslims—followers of the Islamic faith—as are all Mauritanians. They pray five times each day, beginning with the hour before dawn.

The sun as it rises chases darkness from the dunes. They turn from gray to brown to gold, and lose the coolness of the night. The tracks left by small nighttime creatures leave patterns on the sand.

By the time the sky has begun to lighten, Fatimatou's mother is cooking a kind of porridge called *incha* for breakfast. There is also tea, and fresh milk from the family's goats, who spent the night tied to big bushes near the tent.

Now that it is day, Fatimatou and her nephew Sidi untie the goats and send them off to find things to eat. Sometimes they wander very far looking for bushes and small trees to nibble on, but they always return to the tents before nighttime.

Only on a very special occasion, such as a marriage in the family or the feast that marks the end of the holy month of Ramadan, would one of the goats be killed for its meat. Above all, the herd is a source of fresh milk—an essential drink throughout Mauritania—and a sign of a family's well-being.

Years ago, most of Mauritania's people lived as nomads, traveling from place to place with their herds in search of grazing lands. Then came a long period of time when no rain fell at all; no plants grew for the herds to feed on, and there was no water for them to drink. Thousands of animals died during this drought, and many families lost their livelihoods. Now nearly everyone, including Fatimatou's family, has fewer animals than they once did.

Fatimatou (left) *and the family's goat herd*

Fatimatou's father works in the palm groves of Teyarett. He helps to make sure that the system for pumping water to all the palm trees keeps working well. The trees need lots of water all year round so that they'll be full of fruit for the harvest season.

The dress that Fatimatou wears is really one long piece of cloth wrapped in a certain way. It's called a *melaffa,* and she has several in different colors. She keeps them in a suitcase, safe from the sand. Fatimatou and her sister both wear bracelets and necklaces made of multicolored beads. They found these half-buried in the sand near the tents and know that they were once worn by people who lived in the same place a long time ago.

Above: *Fatimatou's sister, her niece, and her father inside the family's tent.*
Left: *Fatimatou stores her clothes in a suitcase.*

15

Far to the south, where the river runs, is the village of M'bagne, where Hamadi and his family live. Their home is really four small houses built all around a big yard. There is room for many people, because Hamadi lives with his parents, brothers, and sisters, and his aunt, uncle, and cousins as well. They use the rooms in the houses for keeping belongings in, for getting dressed, and for sleeping if it's cold or rainy, but everyone spends most of their time outside in the yard or on the shady covered porches.

The earliest hour of the morning here is the noisiest time of day. First, the rooster crowing in one yard is answered by another; then the goats and sheep begin to bleat, the cows low, and the donkeys let out their pealing bray. When Hamadi wakes up, he washes, and then puts his sleeping-mattress away inside the house.

Every morning, a few young boys visit the house, waiting quietly until Hamadi's sisters and cousins offer them some bread and coffee. They are *almube*, students from the religious school nearby. Since they have no relatives in the village, they rely on different families for their meals.

Opposite page: *The village of M'bagne*

Above: *Breakfast at Hamadi's house.*
Left: Almube, *religious students, waiting for breakfast*

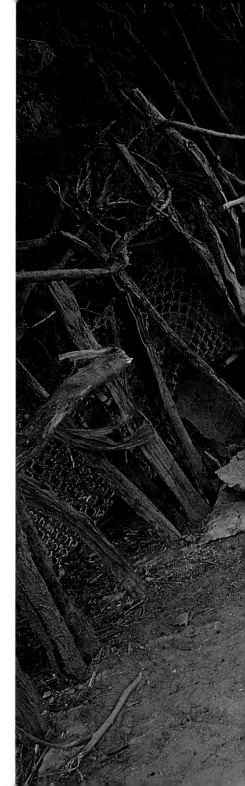

Left: *Hamadi's grandmother Kibbel making yogurt.* Right: *Hamadi (in blue shirt) and his friends walking to school*

Hamadi's family owns animals, too—goats and sheep, two cows, and a calf. Hamadi's grandmother Kibbel uses the goats' milk to make a kind of yogurt called *cossam caddam,* and people from all over the village come to buy it from her. Hamadi and his brother Samba let the goats out of their pen each morning so that they can go outside the village to graze.

After breakfast, Hamadi, his father, and the other children walk together to the school on the other side of the village. Hamadi's father is a teacher there and gives lessons in math and French to the older students.

Hamadi's father teaching class

In the early 1900s, France controlled many parts of North and West Africa, including those that became the countries of Senegal, Mali, and Mauritania. After Mauritania became independent in 1960, certain things introduced by the French remained in use, including the French language and school system. Today, French is still taught in schools and is spoken in the larger towns and cities, although the country's official language is Arabic.

Hamadi's favorite subject is math. He also likes learning French, although at home he always speaks Poular. Someday, Hamadi thinks, he'd like to be a teacher too.

The village school only goes up to a certain level. If older children want to continue studying, they have to go to school in a bigger town, where they can stay with relatives or friends. Right now, mostly only boys leave the village to go on to the next level of school. Most of the girls stay in the village and work in the households and gardens, but this is changing little by little. A few of them go with their brothers to Bogué and study at the *lycée* (upper school) there.

Hamadi (center) *and some of his classmates*

Fatimatou doesn't go to school. When she was smaller, though, she went to the *medersa* in the village nearby and studied the Koran, the Muslim holy book. She learned to read and write Arabic there.

Now, she sometimes studies and practices writing on her own with a *loha*–a wooden tablet inscribed with verses from the Koran. Fatimatou reads out loud from the *loha* in a kind of chant.

Not far from the tents is a well that goes deep down into the earth. All of the water that

Fatimatou's family needs for cooking, drinking, washing, and bathing comes from the well, and Fatimatou makes several trips there every day. Her arms quickly get tired from hauling up buckets of water with the long rope. Then her brother's wife, Safiya, takes her turn, and Fatimatou helps fill the big container and the water-skins, trying not to spill much. People who live in the desert have used these skins, called *guerbas,* for hundreds of years. They keep the water inside cool and fresh for a long time.

While Hamadi and the others are at school, his older sisters Bana and Hadia go to get drinking water from one of the public faucets in the village. They meet many friends there, and greet them while waiting for their turn to fill their buckets. *On m'balijam* means "good morning," but in the Poular language there is a different greeting for nearly every hour of the day! Back at the house, Bana pours the water into great big clay pots on the porch. Like the *guerbas* in the desert, the pots keep the water cool and clean for drinking.

The riverbank is another one of the gathering places of the village. All through the day, women and girls bring loads of clothes to wash. There are shirts, skirts, and long robes called *boubous* in different-colored cloths. After being scrubbed clean and rinsed of soap, the clothes are hung over low bushes on the bank. It doesn't take long for them to dry under the hot sun. Meanwhile, girls wash their hair, children get their baths, and everyone dips into the water to stay cool.

Hamadi's sister Hadia (in blue) carrying water from a public faucet

Above: *Freshly washed clothes drying in the sun.* Below: *A mother bathing her child*

While working around the village, many Halpoular mothers carry their smallest children with them, bundled on their backs. When they are carried like this, the children hardly ever cry.

At the very center of the village is the marketplace. Here, you can buy vegetables, freshly caught fish, cloth, grain, and ready-to-eat snacks. If you're good at bargaining, you can get the best price for what you want to buy.

After buying what they need at the market, Hamadi's sisters and cousins prepare the midday meal. They cook fish and different kinds of vegetables together in a spicy sauce and put it on top of rice. This is what most people in the village eat at lunch, which is the biggest meal of the day. Hamadi and the other children come home from school at noon to eat with their families.

In many Halpoular households, men and women eat separately. Each group has its own big bowl, and everyone sits in a circle around it. After washing their hands, people scoop up little balls of food from the part of the dish that's in front of them. It would be very bad manners to take food from someone else's part of the bowl!

If there is a guest eating with the family, then the best pieces of fish or vegetables are always put right in front of him or her.

Opposite page: *The marketplace in M'bagne.* Above: *Bringing goods back from the market.* Left: *Sharing the midday meal*

Fatimatou, Aichetou, and their brother's wife Safiya always take turns cooking the meals. Lunch is usually rice mixed with spices and bits of dried meat called *tishtar*. But if it's Fatimatou's turn to cook, she likes to make something different. She *especially* likes macaroni, which her father can buy in Atar, the nearest large town. He goes there twice a month, by bush taxi, to buy rice, grain, meat, and vegetables at the big marketplace.

Cooking over a fire is hot and smoky; Fatimatou thinks it would be much easier to use a gas stove like the ones people use in town, but the gas tanks are heavy and hard to bring out to the tents.

Sometimes at lunchtime, Fatimatou's father is working in the palm groves, her mother has gone into the village, and her brother is tending the animals. So Fatimatou and her sister eat their own share and save the rest for when the others come home.

The afternoon is the hottest time of day in the desert, so after lunch everyone finds a shady place and rests until the sun lowers in the sky and the air becomes cooler.

Opposite page: *Aichetou washes her hands before eating.* Above: *Fatimatou and Aichetou eating macaroni for their midday meal*

Above: *Hamadi and his friends playing* ligum. Left: *Handmade toy cars.* Opposite page, left: *A girl plays with her handmade doll.* Right: *Halpoular girls with festive braids*

On his days off from school, Hamadi and his friends like to go swimming or play soccer. Soccer is everyone's favorite sport in Mauritania.

One of the other games Hamadi and his friends play is a lot like hide-and-seek, except that two people are "it." This game is called *tuktukurdu* in the Poular language. There is also *ligum,* which is just like tug-of-war, and a game called *woli* that you play on a long wooden board.

Many Mauritanian children make their own toys, using things that they find. With wire, tin cans, milk cartons, and other things, they make cars and even airplanes and helicopters with wheels and propellers that turn. They make dolls, too, and houses and clothes for them.

When they rest after doing work around the house, Hamadi's sisters and cousins like to take turns braiding each other's hair. Everyday braids don't take too long to make, but braiding for a holiday or celebration can take hours and hours to do. When friends in the village have a party, everyone gets all dressed up; they have fun dancing together and eating snacks such as *beignets,* which are like doughnuts without holes.

When Fatimatou's friends come to visit her, she likes to play long card games with them. But one of the things she and her girlfriends especially love to do is to put henna on each other's hands and feet. They use a soft powder made from the dried leaves of the henna plant and mix it with some water; then they paint it onto their hands and feet in different patterns. For special days, such as weddings, the patterns can be very complicated. The color usually stays bright for two or three weeks before it fades away.

Whenever someone comes to visit Fatimatou or her family, they are offered something to drink right away. Visitors are glad to have some fresh *zrig,* a cool drink made from goat's milk, sugar, and water. Then Fatimatou makes a pot of hot, sweet tea. She pours it slowly into little glasses so that it makes a light, bubbly foam that everyone likes. While catching up on news and relaxing, the visitor drinks three glasses of tea, each one sweeter than the last. The hotter it is outside the tent, the more the tea seems to cool you down.

Above: *Fatimatou and her friend playing cards.*
Right: *Fatimatou always likes to have henna on because she thinks it looks much nicer than bare hands and feet.*

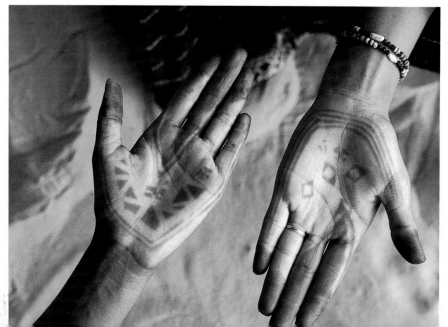

Fatimatou helping to tighten the tent ropes (inset); *a sandstorm in the desert*

In the desert, there are times when the wind blows so hard that the whole tent shakes, and the big poles that hold it in place nearly fall down. When this happens, the ropes that hold the cotton cloth must be tightened, and the poles must be dug more deeply into the sand.

There are days, too, when the wind suddenly stops, and everything is completely still. Fatimatou and her family know that this is the time to get under cover because it means a sandstorm is on the way. They all go into the tent and close down the sides completely. When the sandstorm comes, a great wind rises and the sky turns orange with swirling sand, so that you can hardly see anything at all.

The sandstorm passes quickly. Sometimes a short rainfall follows. Then the sun comes out again, and it's as hot as ever.

To the east of the family's tent is a place unlike other parts of the desert. Fatimatou and her sister love to go there. Sometimes they see their friend the shepherd boy, letting his goats drink from the quiet pool.

Fatimatou smooths out the sand while laying down the hasira.

Left: *A neighbor winds a ball of wool for tentmaking.* Above: *Late afternoon at the tents*

In the evening, Fatimatou smooths out the sand before laying down the *hasira,* making sure there aren't any stones or bumps underneath. Then she and her family and their friends from the nearby tent all sit outside together, talking, relaxing, and drinking *zrig.*

Aichetou prepares a dish of steamed wheat called *couscous* for dinner; their neighbor Maimouna winds the wool that she will weave into tent-trimming. Everyone has a pillow to rest on, and as the sky darkens, they all feel the cool breeze that comes with the evening.

37

Left: *Hadia, holding baby brother Ousmane, sweeps the yard.* Above: *Hamadi shows a friend the pigeon house.* Opposite page: *A mosque in M'bagne*

As the day ends in M'bagne, the women return from their last trip to the river. After bathing baby Ousmane, Hamadi's mother brings the sleeping mattresses out onto the porch and prepares the evening meal. The dish she makes is like the *couscous* eaten by Fatimatou's family, but its Poular name is *lachiri.*

While his sister Hadia sweeps the yard, Hamadi visits his pigeons, who live in a small house he built just for them. Though Samba and his sisters like to look at them, the birds will let only Hamadi pick them up. He speaks to them softly, stroking their wings. When they fly, they never go far, and always come back to their house before night.

As the sky grows darker, Hamadi hears the voice of the *noddinowo* calling out from the tall tower of the mosque. The mosque is the Islamic house of worship, and it is the job of the *noddinowo* to remind people that it's time for their evening prayers. A crescent moon and star stand out against the sky; these are the symbols of Islam.

The dates that grow in the region where Fatimatou lives are considered the best in all of Mauritania.

At a certain time of year, usually around May, it's time for the date harvest. Fatimatou and her family take down their tents and pack up all their things, and her father hires someone with a truck to bring them all into Teyarett. The family has three small houses there, with the rock wall of the valley on one side and the palm grove on the other. The houses are built of branches and palm fronds, so tightly woven together that rain can't come through. Fatimatou and her family live here for about four months each year, until the date-harvesting season is over. Many people come from the big towns to spend time here during the harvest and bring boxes of dates back as gifts for their friends.

Everyone in Fatimatou's family is busy during the harvest season, or *guetna*. Her father and brothers make sure that the water pumps keep working well. Her mother makes strands of sun-dried dates for later, when the *guetna* is over. Fatimatou and her friends help gather the dates, climbing up high to reach the darkest, ripest ones. Some of the dates are sent to the market in Atar to be sold, and some are just for the family to eat.

Dates are Fatimatou's favorite food. She loves eating lots of them during the *guetna, but she often gets toothaches because the dates are so sweet.*

In the village, there's a very small market where people sell bread, meat, and other things, and there's also a little shop where Fatimatou and her friends can buy candy. The woman who runs the shop also knows how to prepare goatskins for making pillows and water-skins; another neighbor weaves rugs out of wool.

When she's living in Teyarett, Fatimatou sees many of her friends who live there all year round. They pick dates together and play in the palm groves. In the evening, they sit outside and sing songs or play cards by flashlight.

But she's still happy when it's time to go back out to the desert again. It's cleaner and quieter there, and the tents are more cool and comfortable than houses are, she thinks.

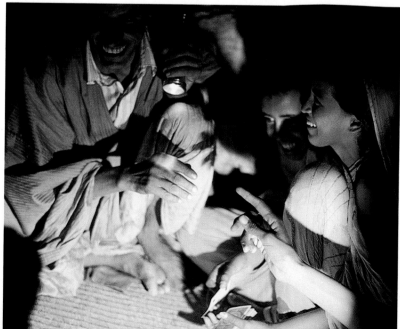

Above: *A neighbor from the village weaving a rug.*
Left: *Fatimatou playing cards with her friends from the village*

43

Below: *Young girls on their way home from the M'bagne gardens.*
Right: *A mother carries her child on her back as she works in the village gardens.*

During the spring and summer months, there is much work to be done in Hamadi's village, too. Most of the women are busy tending crops in the large garden by the river. They grow potatoes, onions, beets and beans, tomatoes, okra, and more. Everyone shares both the work and then the harvest when the vegetables are gathered.

The parts of the riverbank where corn and other crops are planted are called *walo* fields, and they grow with the help of the river water. Further inland, there are places where other kinds of crops are planted; these are called *dieri* fields, and they rely on the rainfall. During the summer, when there's no school, Hamadi's cousin Sileye and the older boys go to work in the *dieri* fields, breaking up the hard soil so it will be ready for planting. But if there is no rain, then the fields will stay barren and dry.

Left: Walo *fields along the river in M'bagne.* Below: *Sileye and friends on their way to the* dieri *fields*

When they are working in the fields, they have to watch out for the small scorpions that hide under rocks and can sting with their quick forked tails. Sileye was stung once, and the pain went all the way up his leg. His family took him to see a *marabout,* a religious man who knows traditional ways of healing. The *marabout* gave Sileye something for the sting that made the pain go away in one day.

Left: *Downtown Nouak-chott.* Below: *A Nouak-chott neighborhood where many migrants live*

During the summer vacation, Hamadi's father goes to visit family and friends who live in Nouakchott, Mauritania's largest city. Many people who used to live in the countryside herding animals or farming, now live in Nouakchott and other cities and towns. Thousands left their lands during the terrible drought of the 1970s, when their animals died and no crops could grow. These migrants hoped that they would be able to find work and a new way of life in the towns, since the old way of life had become impossible for them. So many families have moved to Nouakchott that parts of the city are overcrowded with the small houses and shacks that they built for themselves.

In Nouakchott, both men and women work in traditional and nontraditional jobs—as artisans, technicians, and secretaries, as shopkeepers or street vendors. Still, as more and more people leave their villages to come live in the city, it becomes harder to find any sort of job at all.

Above: *A Nouakchott woman learning computer skills.* Below: *A woman working at a rug factory in Nouakchott*

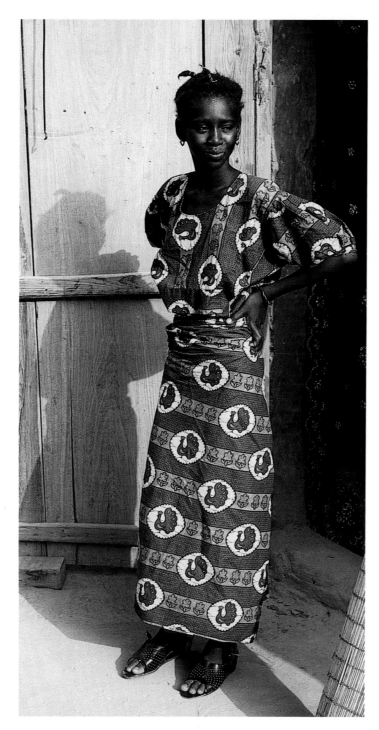

When Hamadi's father returned from Nouakchott, he brought gifts for everyone. For Hamadi, there was a new shirt and other clothes, and for his mother, a fine dress. Hadia loved her gift—a shining new pair of shoes.

Soon it will be time for school to begin again. Soon, too, it will be time for the fishermen to cast their nets into the river and draw in loads of quick, flashing fish. In preparation, they make sure that their nets are strong and mend any holes there might be. But there has still been no harvest from the *dieri* fields, for the rain has not come.

One late summer day, the sound of chanting voices and clapping hands travels through the village. A group of women, including Hamadi's grandmother Kibbel, is marching toward the river, singing *"bayna mohammedu!"* and asking God to send rain to help the crops grow. They carry branches of trees in their hands and wear baskets for gathering the harvested corn on their heads like hats. Hamadi and many other children join them as they go along, singing.

When they come to the river, the women smear wet earth on their faces, and many people jump into the water, feeling happy and hopeful that the rain will come.

Usually, after the women sing *bayna mohammedu,* the rain comes within a few days.

Opposite page: *Hamadi's sister Maimouna watches a fisherman make a net.* Left and below: *Singing "bayna mohammedu," village women march to the river.*

The date harvest is over, and Fatimatou's family has moved back out to the desert. One afternoon, Sidi sees something moving along the dunes beyond the tents. It's a herd of camels, one of the biggest he has ever seen, traveling slowly across the valley. They move from one *titarik* bush to another, nibbling the tender tops. Fatimatou's father comes to say hello to the camel herder and exchange news with him. The herder says that he is taking the camels up to the northern city of Nouadhibou, where they will be sold. He thinks that the trip will take about sixteen days. One very big camel, the leader of the herd, carries all of the man's baggage on its back —everything he will need for the journey.

Left: *Fatimatou's father greets the camel herder.*

Opposite page: *Fatimatou's nephew Sidi watches a camel herd.* Right: *The lead camel grazing*

That evening, when the shepherd boy returns with his herds, he helps write a letter to Fatimatou's oldest brother Brahim, who works up north. Fatimatou makes tea by the light of a gas lamp; by the time the last glass is finished, the stars have come out. The sound of voices talking low comes over from the other tents; then quiet falls as night comes.

Far to the south, as the sky grows dark, Hamadi hears the voice of the *noddinowo* calling out from the tall tower of the mosque. As the chant ends, Hamadi and his brothers and sisters begin their own song, softly, clapping their hands until it's time for the smallest ones to sleep.